MY FIRST BOOK

UKRAINE

ALL ABOUT UKRAINE FOR KIDS

GL BED
CHILDREN BOOKS

Interior and cover Design: Daniel Day

Editor: Margaret Bam

For My Sons, Daniel, David and Jude

Kiev, Ukraine

Ukraine

Ukraine is a **country**.

A country is land that is controlled by a **single government**. Countries are also called **nations, states, or nation-states**.

Countries can be **different sizes**. Some countries are big and others are small.

St Michael's Cathedral, Kiev, Ukraine

Where Is Ukraine?

Ukraine is located in the continent of Europe.

A continent is a massive area of land that is separated from others by water or other natural features.

Ukraine is situated in Eastern Europe.

The Victoria Film Studios in Kyiv

Capital

The capital of Ukraine is Kyiv which is also spelled Kiev.

Kyiv is located in the **central part** of the country.

Kyiv is the largest city in Ukraine.

St Vladimir's Cathedral, Ukraine

Oblasts

Ukraine is a country that is divided into 24 oblasts.

The oblasts of Ukraine are as follows:

Cherkasy, Chernihiv, Chernivtsi, Dnipropetrovsk, Donetsk, Ivano-Frankivsk, Kharkiv, Kherson, Khmelnytskyi, Kiev, Kirovohrad, Luhansk, Lviv, Mykolaiv, Odessa, Poltava, Rivne, Sumy, Ternopil, Vinnytsia, Volyn, Zakarpattia, Zaporizhia, and Zhytomyr.

Pokrovsky Monastery, Kyiv

Population

Ukraine has population of around **43 million people** making it the 36th most populated country in the world and the seventh most populated country in Europe.

Size

Ukraine is **603,628 square kilometres** making it the second largest country in Europe by area.

Ukraine is 45th largest country in the world.

Languages

The official language of Ukraine is Ukrainian. Historical linguists trace the origin of the Ukrainian language to Old East Slavic.

Ukrainian is spoken by around 40 million people.

Here are a few Ukrainian phrases
- **Добрий день!** - Hello
- **Ласкаво просимо!** - Welcome

Bogdan Khmelnitsky Statue

Attractions

There are lots of interesting places to see in Ukraine.

Some beautiful places to visit in Ukraine are

- St. Sophia's Cathedral
- Kiev Pechersk Lavra
- St. Michael's Golden-Domed Monastery
- Potemkin Stairs
- Ukrainian Motherland Monument
- Golden Gate

Kiev, Ukraine

History of Ukraine

People have lived in Ukraine for a very long time. It is believed that humans have inhabited Ukraine from as early as 32,000 BC.

From the 14th to the 18th century, portions of Ukraine were ruled by Lithuania, Russia, and Poland.

After World War I and the Russian Revolution of 1917, most of Ukraine became a republic of the Soviet Union. Ukraine gained independence in 1991 when the Soviet Union dissolved.

Motherland Monument in Kyiv

Customs in Ukraine

Ukraine has many fascinating customs and traditions.

- **Christmas Eve's Kolyadkas (carols) play a very integral part of Christmas celebrations in Ukraine. Kolyadnyky (carolers) visit the houses of neighbours, singing carols, and wishing prosperity and health to all family members.**
- **Many Ukrainians put bread and salt on the table when guests visit.**

Donetsk, Ukraine

Music of Ukraine

There are many different music genres in Ukraine such as **Russian pop, Classical music, Opera, Pop, Rock, Folk and Jazz.**

Some notable Ukrainian musicians include
- **Jamala**
- **DakhaBrakha**
- **Okean Elzy**
- **Svyatoslav Vakarchuk**
- **Max Barskih**
- **Ruslana**
- **Ani Lorak**

Borscht

Food of Ukraine

Ukraine is known for having delicious, flavoursome and rich dishes.

The national dish of Ukraine is borscht, which is a delicious beet soup.

Food of Ukraine

Some popular dishes in Ukraine include

- **Paska**
- **Varenyky**
- **Holubtsi**
- **Holodets**
- **Deruni**
- **Chicken Kyiv**
- **Nalesniki**

Kirove, Ukraine

Weather in Ukraine

Ukraine has a temperate climate with a sufficient amount of sunshine and year-round rainfall.

The warmest months fall between **May to August.**

Verkhovyna, Ukraine

Animals of Ukraine

There are many wonderful animals in Ukraine. There are around 350 species of birds, more than 100 species of mammals, and more than 200 species of fish.

Here are some animals that live in Ukraine

- **Wolves**
- **Wildcats**
- **Wildpigs**
- **Martens**
- **Rodents**

Sumy, Ukraine

Beaches

There are many beautiful beaches in Ukraine which is one of the reasons why so many people visit this beautiful country every year.

Here are some of Ukraine's beaches

- Arcadia
- Langeron
- Koblevo
- Berdyansk
- Kyrylivka

Ukrainian Flag

Sports of Ukraine

Sports play an integral part in Ukraine culture. The most popular sport is **Football.**

Here are some of famous sportspeople from Ukraine

- **Sergey Bubka - Pole Vault**
- **Oleksandr Usyk - Boxer**
- **Vasiliy Lomachenko - Boxer**
- **Yevhen Konoplyanka - Football**
- **Vitali Klitschko - Boxer**
- **Wladimir Klitschko - Boxer**

Lviv, Ukraine

Famous

Many successful people hail from Ukraine.

Here are some notable Ukraine figures

- **Milla Jovovich – Actress**
- **Yulia Tymoshenko – Politician**
- **Volodymyr Zelenskyy – Politician**
- **Mila Kunis – Actress**
- **Gennadiy Bogolyubov – Businessman**

Vorokhta, Ukraine

Something Extra...

As a little something extra, we are going to share some lesser known facts about Ukraine.

- **Ukraine is home to the second-deepest subway station in the world.**
- **Ukraine is the birthplace of Easter Eggs.**
- **Ukraine is the world's largest producer of sunflower seeds.**

Words From the Author

We hope that you enjoyed learning about the wonderful country of Ukraine.

Ukraine is a country rich in culture and beauty, with lots of wonderful places to visit and people to meet.

We hope you continue to learn more about this wonderful nation. If you enjoyed this book, consider leaving a review!

With Love

Printed in Great Britain
by Amazon

17648364R00027